LEADERSHIP
· SKILLS ·
FOR WOMEN

Better Management Skills

This highly popular range of inexpensive paperbacks covers all areas of basic management. Practical, easy to read and instantly accessible, these guides will help managers to improve their business or communication skills. Those marked * are available on audio cassette.

The books in this series can be tailored to specific company requirements. For further details, please contact the publisher, Kogan Page, telephone 0171 278 0433, fax 0171 837 6348.

Be a Successful Supervisor
Business Etiquette
Coaching Your Employees
Consulting for Success
Creative Decision-making
Creative Thinking in Business
Delegating for Results
Effective Meeting Skills
Effective Performance Appraisals*
Effective Presentation Skills
Empowerment
First Time Supervisor
Get Organised!
Goals and Goal Setting
How to Communicate
  Effectively*
How to Develop a Positive
  Attitude
How to Develop Assertiveness
How to Motivate People*
How to Understand Financial
  Statements
How to Write a Staff Manual
Improving Employee Performance
Improving Relations at Work
Keeping Customers for Life

Leadership Skills for Women
Learning to Lead
Make Every Minute Count*
Managing Disagreement
  Constructively
Managing Organisational Change
Managing Part-Time Employees
Managing Quality Customer
  Service
Managing Your Boss
Marketing for Success
Memory Skills in Business
Mentoring
Office Management
Productive Planning
Project Management
Quality Customer Service
Rate Your Skills as a Manager
Self-Managing Teams
Selling Professionally
Speed Reading in Business
Successful Negotiation
Successful Telephone Techniques
Systematic Problem-solving
Team Building
Training Methods that Work

LEADERSHIP
· SKILLS ·
FOR WOMEN

**Marilyn Manning and
Patricia Haddock**

KOGAN
PAGE

First published in the United States of America in 1989
by Crisp Publications Inc, 95 First Street,
Los Altos, California 94022, USA

This edition first published in Great Britain in 1989
by Kogan Page Ltd, 120 Pentonville Road, London N1 9JN

Reprinted 1991, 1992, 1995

British Library Cataloguing in Publication Data

Manning, Marilyn
  Leadership skills for women.
  1. Women managers. Leadership
  I. Title   II. Haddock, Patricia
  658.4'092'088042

  ISBN 0–7494–0059–5
  ISBN 0–7494–0060–9 pbk

Typeset by DP Photosetting, Aylesbury, Bucks
Printed and bound in Great Britain by
Biddles Ltd, Guildford and King's Lynn

Contents

To the Reader

You have worked long and hard to reach your present position. In the process, you have observed successful leaders in action. The chances are that you have formed opinions of what makes leaders effective or ineffective.

People don't develop leadership skills by waving a magic wand or reciting the perfect word. No one becomes a good leader overnight.

The seeds of good leadership come from a combination of personal skills, talent, and character. You shape and nurture your leadership style by strengthening your talents, working to eliminate problem behaviours, and learning to develop new, more productive ones.

So, why in this book, have we concentrated on female leaders?

Everything you have learned, absorbed, and observed over your lifetime has influenced your behaviour. This means that gender and gender-specific behaviour plays a part in your leadership style. This book will show you how to use your unique talents, *plus* your feminine strengths, to become the best leader possible, both on the job and in your personal life.

Marilyn Manning
Patricia Haddock

About This Book

Leadership Skills for Women is not like most books. It has a unique 'self-paced' format that encourages a reader to become personally involved. Designed to be 'read with a pencil', there is an abundance of exercises, activities, assessments and cases that invite participation.

The objective of *Leadership Skills for Women* is to provide information that will help a reader understand the qualities that make people leaders, and then teach basic leadership skills that can be applied in the workplace. The emphasis is on women and the book addresses unique challenges and opportunities women leaders face.

Leadership Skills for Women can be used effectively in a number of ways. Here are some possibilities:

Self-study. Because the book is self-instructional, all that is needed is a quiet place, some time and a pencil. By completing the activities and exercises, a reader should not only receive valuable feedback, but also practical steps for self-improvement.

Workshops and seminars. The book is ideal for assigned reading prior to a workshop or seminar. With the basics in hand, the quality of the participation will improve, and more time can be spent on concept extensions and applications. The book is also effective when it is distributed at the beginning of a session, and participants work through the contents.

Open learning. Books can be sent to those not able to attend group training sessions.

CHAPTER 1
The Characteristics of Effective Leaders

'Take responsibility, and people will *give* you responsibility. Take responsibility for your health and well-being. Take responsibility for your work. Take responsibility for your life, the good *and* the bad. Take responsibility and you take the lead! Be the kind of person people can count on – and it will pay off.'

Daniel Meacham
The Magic of Self-Confidence

'Manager' and 'supervisor' are labels that are often used interchangeably in job descriptions. You may carry either title, but neither automatically makes you a leader.

The title of 'leader' must be earned by inspiring and motivating people to give their best. A successful leader commits herself to her organisation and fosters that same kind of commitment in her followers.

The successful leader:

● knows her job and her field thoroughly;
● stays on top of current developments, trends, and theories;
● knows her people, including their strengths, weaknesses, hopes, and goals;
● shares a vision of service, excellence, and achievement with others;
● demonstrates by her words and actions a strength of character.

Characteristics of:

A LEADER	A FOLLOWER
Good listener	Good talker
Accessible	Hard to find
Decisive	Avoids decisions
Gracious	Self-promoting
Keeps it simple	Makes it complicated
Optimistic	Pessimistic
Gives credit	Takes credit
Confronts problems	Avoids problems
Speaks directly	Manipulates
Acknowledges mistakes	Blames others
Says 'Yes'	Explains why it can't be done
Enthusiastic	Placid
Seeks strong subordinates	Seeks weak subordinates
Positive attitude	Negative attitude

Test your leadership potential

	Usually	Sometimes	Seldom
1. I look for positive challenges during periods of change.	_____	_____	_____
2. I'm willing to take risks and learn from mistakes.	_____	_____	_____
3. I regularly acknowledge others' accomplishments.	_____	_____	_____
4. I reflect the values I claim to believe in.	_____	_____	_____
5. I look for ways to share power.	_____	_____	_____
6. I delegate tasks with authority and decisiveness.	_____	_____	_____

	Usually	Sometimes	Seldom
7. I have written long-term plans and I am committed to them.	_____	_____	_____
8. I know how to motivate other people.	_____	_____	_____
9. I know how to promote team effort and spirit.	_____	_____	_____
10. I regularly give honest, constructive feedback to my team.	_____	_____	_____
11. I make decisions promptly.	_____	_____	_____

Striving to answer 'Usually' to each of these questions is a worthy goal for any leader. Any questions you answered with 'Sometimes' or 'Seldom' should become your goals as you study this book.

List your leadership goals below. For instance, 'I will look for opportunities to be more decisive.'

Goal 1.

Goal 2.

Goal 3.

Goal 4.

Goal 5.

Many 'styles' of leadership

There are as many leadership styles as there are leaders. Many will work, but some are more effective than others.

Generally, an effective leadership style will allow you to:

- identify and target realistic and relevant goals;
- produce realistic and relevant results;

- align your goals to stated business objectives;
- design performance requirements that are based on measurable items such as quality, quantity, cost, timeliness, and profit;
- revise plans as necessary;
- keep lines of communication open.

To the extent that any management style hinders you, it is ineffective and should be changed.

What style are you?

As you read through the following characteristics of leadership styles, circle with a <u>blue</u> pen those attributes that describe you. Then go over the items you circled in blue and mark with a <u>yellow</u> highlighter any characteristics you believe may be detrimental to your effectiveness. Finally, read the lists again and circle with a <u>red</u> pen attributes you think would be beneficial for you to develop.

After you finish this exercise, you should have a clear picture of your current leadership assets and liabilities. Using what you have recorded, you can put together a plan to become a more effective leader.

You may find it helpful to observe the work styles of your employees and adjust your style accordingly. This is called 'situational leadership' and it can be very powerful. For example, when you approach an 'analytical' employee, you should prepare details and communicate in a highly methodical way. If your style is naturally different (for instance, if you are 'charismatic') your enthusiasm and need to persuade might make you ineffective leading an 'analyser'. You will have many opportunities to recognise and practise situational leadership throughout this book.

There are two primary leadership styles for women: quiet or outgoing.

For a good book on how to align employee performance with goals, read *Effective Performance Appraisals* by Robert B Maddux (Kogan Page).

Style 1: *Quiet styles*

Traditional team player		Analytical problem solver	
The Supporter		**The Perfectionist**	
Major flaw: Agrees too much		Major flaw: Questions too much	
Likeable	Helpful	Conscientious	Reserved
Easygoing	Patient	Fretful	Mature
Deliberate	Calm	Perfectionist	Systematic
Low-risk taker	Loyal	Accurate	High standards
Predictable	Team player	Self-disciplined	Orderly

Style 2: *Outgoing styles*

Dominant, controlling		Charismatic motivator	
The Director		**The Motivator**	
Major flaw: Directs too much		Major flaw: Talks too much	
Direct	Risk-taking	Enthusiastic	Influential
Organiser	Energising	Sympathetic	Generous
Self-confident	Fast-thinking	Gregarious	Friendly
Responsible	Forceful	Social	Dramatic
Powerful	Ambitious	Loves recognition	Charismatic

A leader's attitude affects productivity

'Your attitude speaks so loudly, employees can't hear what you say.'

Elwood N Chapman

Your attitude as a leader will set the pace and tone for your employees. People tend to mirror each other, and employees especially tend to mirror their managers.

If your attitude is positive and dynamic, people you work with will reflect your attitude by becoming more positive and dynamic.

If, however, you complain and play the victim, you will find yourself surrounded by reflections of yourself.

Your attitude also will affect your department's productivity. When you develop good relationships with your employees and consistently project a positive attitude, they will tend to respond to that by being more productive.

But no one can be upbeat all the time. Sometimes personal problems, health problems, and people problems all seem to conspire to erode our positive feeling and attitude.

Following are some tips to help you keep your attitude positive, especially during those 'down' times:*

- Engage in a regular exercise programme.
- Inject humour into your life and your workplace.
- Break major goals into smaller, more easily attainable ones.
- Take frequent, short breaks during the day for renewal.
- Balance work and leisure more effectively.
- Try volunteering to add perspective and depth to your life.
- Keep yourself looking professional.
- Find someone you trust as a role model, confidante, and sounding board.

Leadership exercise

Rate your current attitude. Read each statement and circle the number you feel represents where you belong on the attitude scale. If you circle a 10, you are saying your attitude cannot be improved in this area; if you circle a 1, you are saying your attitude could not be worse. Be honest.

---

*Adapted from *How to Develop a Positive Attitude* by Elwood N Chapman (Kogan Page).

	High (Positive)					*Low* (Negative)			

1. My feeling is that my boss would currently rate my attitude as: 10 9 8 7 6 5 4 3 2 1

2. Given the same choice, my colleagues would rate my attitude as: 10 9 8 7 6 5 4 3 2 1

3. Given the same choice, my family would rate my attitude as: 10 9 8 7 6 5 4 3 2 1

4. Given the same choice, my employees would rate my attitude as: 10 9 8 7 6 5 4 3 2 1

5. Realistically, I would rate my attitude as: 10 9 8 7 6 5 4 3 2 1

6. My effectiveness level is: 10 9 8 7 6 5 4 3 2 1

7. My creativity level is: 10 9 8 7 6 5 4 3 2 1

8. My enthusiasm towards my job is: 10 9 8 7 6 5 4 3 2 1

9. My enthusiasm towards my life is: 10 9 8 7 6 5 4 3 2 1

10. My recent disposition – the patience and sensitivity I show to others – deserves a rating of: 10 9 8 7 6 5 4 3 2 1

Your TOTAL score:

A score of 90 or more is a signal that your attitude is 'in tune' and no adjustments seem necessary; a score between 70 and 89 indicates that minor adjustments may help; a rating between 50 and 69 suggests a major adjustment; if you rated yourself below 50, a complete overhaul may be required.

A leader's attitude and vision

'Attitudes are caught, not taught.'

Elwood N Chapman

Regardless of style, all business leaders take the role of manager and add a 'plus' factor to it. That 'plus' factor is called vision.

Your vision

Your vision should dovetail and support your organisation's goals and/or mission statement. You communicate vision by stating it simply, understandably, and inspirationally. Write it down. Publish it for others to see. Tie it into job descriptions, assignments and performance plans, work, individual and departmental goals. Never let your people forget the common vision they share.

A leader with vision is a person who:

- inspires and motivates;
- projects into the future and communicates a global outlook;
- obtains significant, often extraordinary, results from people;
- is highly committed to excellence, honesty, and productivity;
- is an effective listener.

Take a few minutes to think about your work-related vision and then summarise it in the space provided opposite. You will have an opportunity to review and revise what you have written at the end of this book.

My vision is: _____

_____

_____

_____

_____

_____

_____

_____

_____

_____

_____

_____

_____

_____

_____

_____

_____

_____

_____

_____

_____

_____

_____

_____

_____

Defining your values helps you to support your vision.

Draw a vertical line down the middle of a piece of paper. On one side, list the values you wish to promote.

Now think back to your actions during the past month (refer to your diaries and memos to assist you in recalling actions you took). Then in the other column, write the actions you took that demonstrated your personal commitment to your values.

Example:

Values I promote:	Actions I take:
Open, honest communication	I completed a written performance evaluation for Jack Roberts on 15 March and reviewed it with him in a face-to-face meeting. (*Note.* I do this for each of my employees every six months.)

Add your own:

Values I promote:	Actions I take:

Identifying a leadership model

Think about and respond in writing to the following statements and questions:

1. I consider _____ to be a good leader.
   (NAME)

2. The following qualities make this person a good leader: ____
   _____ .

3. I display the following similar qualities to _____ .
   (NAME)

4. I do not display the following similar qualities to _____ .
   (NAME)

5. I consider my greatest, most unique talents to be: _____
   _____ .

6. What can I learn about effective leadership by studying the
   leadership style of _____ identified in statement 1?
   (NAME)

Leadership exercise
1. Think about a successful leadership experience you have had.
   Select one of your best experiences. Get a vivid image of it.
   Describe it fully:

   (a) Where and when did it take place? Who initiated it?

   (b) Who was involved? What was your role? What were the
   results?

   (c) What motivated you to assume leadership? What risks, if
   any, did you take?

   (d) What were your initial feelings? What did you feel during
   the project and at its end?

   (e) How did you foster cooperation? Keep up enthusiasm?

   (f) How did you lead by example? Communicate your
   values?

(g) Would the leadership model you identified in the previous exercise have done anything differently? Better?

2. Write a few words that best describe your experience, how you felt, what you learned about leadership style and practice, and what you feel to be the single most important factor in your success.

3. Now identify what you feel you need to do or learn to improve your performance.

Prejudices against women as leaders

Despite significant inroads made by the feminist and equal opportunities movements, women still face unspoken prejudices in the workplace. Sometimes these prejudices come to the foreground when a woman assumes a leadership role. You must be aware of these prejudices in order to ensure that you will not act in ways that confirm them.

Some typical prejudices include a belief in the following stereotypes. Tick any you have personally observed or experienced.

Stereotypes

I have experienced or witnessed the belief stated by others that:

☐ Women fall apart when the going gets tough.

☐ Women are catty or love to gossip.

☐ Women are afraid to make decisions or always change their minds.

☐ Women are too picky.

☐ Women use sex to get what they want.

☐ Women can be pushy and loudmouthed.

☐ Women are difficult to work for.

☐ Women aren't able to see the broad view.

☐ Women take things too personally.

☐ Women aren't good team players.

☐ Women are too soft to make decisions.

☐ Women allow their families or personal lives to get in the way of the job.

☐ Women no sooner get trained than they leave to have a baby.

☐ Women are too emotional and cry too easily.

☐ Women can't travel on business because of personal and family commitments.

☐ Women make things more complicated than they really are.

☐ Women are moody, especially at a certain time of the month.

☐ Women are inconsistent and fickle and don't know what they want.

Do you foster any of these stereotypes by your personal behaviour? If so, what steps can you take to change the perception that these stereotypes convey about you?

List any stereotypes that might relate to you and then develop action steps to change your behaviour.

Example:
Stereotype: I can't make up my mind.
Resolution: I will act more decisively.

Add your own:

Stereotype:
Resolution:

Stereotype:
Resolution:

Stereotype:
Resolution:

Working with men

In a recent survey conducted by the authors, more than 100 women managers were asked what advice they would give to potential women managers about working effectively with men. Here's what they said:

1. *Physical appearance makes a difference.* A crisp, no-nonsense image helps to establish positive contact with men. Wear business-like clothing and sensible heels that increase your height.
2. *Be prepared and organised.* Use strong, direct language and stand firm when you are interrupted. Statistics show that women allow themselves to be interrupted 50 per cent more often than men. Don't contribute to those statistics.
3. *Do not overuse hand gestures.* This can detract from what you are saying and may weaken your power position. Men usually use less body language than women. Watch their body language to see how they do it.
4. *Do not flirt.* Keep your conversation directed to the business at hand.
5. *Keep your sense of humour.* A sense of humour helps keep you 'human'.
6. *Don't try to be 'one of the boys'.* If any language or conversation offends, say so.
7. *Depersonalise what men say or do around you.* Many men don't know how to act naturally around businesswomen.
8. *Don't bare your soul by talking about feelings* (especially with casual acquaintances). Most men don't feel comfortable, or can't, handle intensely personal revelations from associates.
9. *Don't feel you have to like someone to get the job done.* Concentrate on the job at hand and productivity, not personalities.
10. *Don't be afraid to ask questions or for advice.* No one has all the answers and honesty is the best approach.

Some men are easier to work with than others.

CHAPTER 2
Leading Your Team

'Example is not the main thing in influencing others. It is the only thing.'

Albert Schweitzer

Women sometimes avoid seeking leadership because they think that leaders are lonely and exposed to risk.

That image is false. Every leader has followers who provide support and reinforce decisions. The business leader leads her team towards one goal: getting the job done in a timely, positive, and cost-effective way.

As a leader, you should inspire the best efforts of your team in order to meet your organisation's goals.

Rate yourself as an effective team builder

The following attitudes support team building. This scale will help identify your strengths, and determine areas where improvements would be beneficial. Circle the number that best reflects where you fall on the scale. The higher the number the more the characteristic describes you. When you have finished, total the numbers circled.

1. When I select employees I choose those who can meet the job requirements and work well with others. 7 6 5 4 3 2

2. I give employees a sense of ownership by involving them in goal setting, problem-solving, and productivity improvement activities. 7 6 5 4 3 2

3. I try to provide team spirit by encouraging people to work together and to support one another. 7 6 5 4 3 2

4. I talk with people openly and honestly and encourage the same kind of communication in return. 7 6 5 4 3 2

5. I keep agreements with my people. 7 6 5 4 3 2

6. I help team members get to know each other so they can learn to trust, respect, and appreciate individual talent and ability. 7 6 5 4 3 2

7. I ensure that employees have the required training to do their jobs. 7 6 5 4 3 2

8. I understand that conflict within groups is normal, but I work to resolve it quickly and fairly before it can become destructive. 7 6 5 4 3 2

9. I believe people will perform as a team when they know what is expected and what benefits they will accrue. 7 6 5 4 3 2

10. I am willing to replace members who cannot or will not meet reasonable standards after appropriate coaching. 7 6 5 4 3 2

TOTAL

A score between 60 and 70 indicates a positive attitude towards people and the type of attitude needed to build and maintain a strong team. A score between 40 and 59 is acceptable and with reasonable effort, team building should be possible for you. If you scored below 40, you need to carefully examine your attitude.

Characteristics of highly cohesive teams

Regardless of the situation or work environment, effective teams demonstrate certain common characteristics. Leaders need to develop these characteristics in their teams. An effective leader makes sure that:

- Team members understand and share the leader's vision.
- Group members respect and ideally like one another.
- Individuals derive satisfaction from being a member of the team.
- Communication is open and all members are encouraged to participate in discussions and, where possible, decision-making.
- The group has a sense of team pride.
- There is little conflict on the team, and when conflict occurs, it is handled using constructive problem-solving techniques.
- Group members are encouraged to cooperate with each other.
- Group decision-making and problem-solving are commonly practised.
- The group learns to work together in a relaxed fashion.
- Team recognition and credit for a good job is freely given.
- Team members understand and share goals, objectives, and mission.

In view of the characteristics outlined above, briefly write your answers to the following questions:

How would you rate your team?

Adapted from *Team Building: An Exercise in Leadership* by Robert B Maddux (Kogan Page).

What are your team's strengths?

What are your team's weaknesses?

What can you do to improve your team?

Seven basics of team leadership

As the leader of your team, you must ensure that the mood of your group is consistently upbeat and the activities it pursues are productive.

Seven ways to help accomplish this are listed below. Tick each that you currently do.

I make every effort to:

- ☐ 1. Treat all employees equally and give each personal attention as required.
- ☐ 2. Keep the promises I make to all team members.
- ☐ 3. Be consistent and act positively, even if I feel negatively.
- ☐ 4. Set a good example and support company policies and procedures.
- ☐ 5. Stay calm. I understand that others tend to imitate a leader's reactions under pressure.
- ☐ 6. Provide opportunities to meet and exchange ideas with my team members.
- ☐ 7. Make sure all my goals are clearly communicated and understood.

If you find yourself guilty of not following any of the above basics, take time to decide how to remedy the situation. Leadership, like any other skill, can be continually improved through practice, practice, practice!

Characteristics of team members

Each member of any team has individual strengths and weaknesses. As a team leader, you must learn to use your team's attributes to get the job done as efficiently as possible.

You also have your personal characteristics which need to be considered. Use the information you discovered earlier about your style of leadership (page 14) and then apply similar characteristics to your team players. You can best motivate your team to perform when assignments match personalities.

The traditional team player

- prefers a secure situation
- is drawn to close relationships
- changes slowly
- is predictable
- is patient
- likes to identify with the company
- supports the status quo
- is possessive
- looks for loyalty
- likes an easygoing, relaxed atmosphere
- views the team as important.

The analytical team player

- likes established operating procedures
- does not like sudden change
- believes that precision works
- is accurate at all costs
- has very high standards for self and others
- tends to worry
- is conventional
- tends to hold back opinions unless certain they are right
- is very conscientious
- is a slow decision-maker
- takes a rational, problem-solving approach to tasks.

The dominating team player

- likes prestige and position
- is easily bored
- likes challenge and change
- measures worth in terms of accomplishments
- likes direct answers from others
- does not like to be controlled by others
- has high self-assurance
- is very assertive and decisive
- is a good risk-taker
- plays a game to win
- is quick and impatient
- is forceful and demanding.

The charismatic team player

- thrives on popularity and social recognition
- likes freedom from detail and control
- uses intuition well
- is sympathetic
- is friendly
- uses verbal skills well
- is trusting
- is good at persuading and charming people
- acts impulsively and emotionally
- is confident and comfortable with self-promotion
- is enthusiastic.

Evaluate your team players

With the team player characteristics just described in mind, list your team members and their individual styles on the form opposite:

Name	His/her preferred workstyle	How to assign tasks
Example: Jim	Dominating	Provide a variety of challenges. Don't oversupervise. Give breathing space.
1.		
2.		
3.		
4.		
5.		
6.		
7.		
8.		

What motivates your team?

Below are some factors employees mention as motivational. Complete this exercise for yourself and each of your employees. If any additional item motivates you or an employee, add it in the space provided.

Motivator	*Motivates* Me	Employee A	Employee B	*Motivates* Employee C	Employee D	Employee E
Financial security	___	___	___	___	___	___
Individual respect	___	___	___	___	___	___
Good work environment	___	___	___	___	___	___
Likes fellow employees	___	___	___	___	___	___
Promotion possibilities	___	___	___	___	___	___
Challenging work	___	___	___	___	___	___
Good benefits	___	___	___	___	___	___
Believes job is important to organisation	___	___	___	___	___	___
Management is fair	___	___	___	___	___	___
Job encourages creativity	___	___	___	___	___	___
Recognition	___	___	___	___	___	___
Opportunities for decision-making	___	___	___	___	___	___

Motivator	*Motivates* Me	Employee A	Employee B	*Motivates* Employee C	Employee D	Employee E
Good feedback because of regular performance plans and ratings	___	___	___	___	___	___
Job freedom	___	___	___	___	___	___
Opportunity for growth and advancement	___	___	___	___	___	___
Manager is hard-working, honest, and fair	___	___	___	___	___	___
___	___	___	___	___	___	___

Strategies for motivating team players

Now that you have identified what motivates your employees, test your abilities to use these motivators.

I feel that I:	Usually	Sometimes	Seldom
Am flexible.	___	___	___
Listen to complaints and ideas objectively.	___	___	___
Find ways to recognise and reward good work.	___	___	___
Provide regular sources of information.	___	___	___
Strive to improve working conditions.	___	___	___

I feel that I:	Usually	Sometimes	Seldom
Involve everyone, when appropriate, in decision-making.	_____	_____	_____
Provide opportunities for advancement.	_____	_____	_____
Build loyalty to the organisation.	_____	_____	_____
Praise good performance in public and counsel poor performers privately.	_____	_____	_____
Nurture a sense of shared values among team players.	_____	_____	_____
Provide feedback, using performance appraisals as motivational devices.	_____	_____	_____
Share my knowledge.	_____	_____	_____
Make sure each person feels important.	_____	_____	_____

Score 3 for a 'Usually', a 2 for a 'Sometimes', and a 1 for a 'Seldom'. If your score is between 33 and 39, congratulations! You have excellent motivational techniques. If you scored between 26 and 32, you are headed in the right direction. If you scored less than 26, you need to significantly improve your motivational techniques before you can call yourself a leader.

CHAPTER 3
Planning Tools

'One intense hour is worth a dreamy day.'

Mary Kay Ash

If it isn't written, it isn't a goal.

Goals

Goals are the outcomes you want to achieve. Every successful leader has them. Properly established goals will allow you to move towards your vision. For this to occur, goals must:

- be clearly stated and attainable;
- be measurable;
- be realistic;
- have deadlines;
- require action steps for each goal; prioritise them;
- be revised and changed as necessary.

Goal setting

In order to achieve your goals, you must have a clear picture of what they entail.

Goal setting is a tool that helps you to accomplish the results you want. Goals should be big enough and exciting enough to challenge you, but not so big or challenging that they become intimidating and unattainable.

Define each of your goals exactly, describing the what, where, when, why and how of each goal. Make each goal so clear, it becomes a verbal photograph of what you want to achieve.

Don't just say you want to be a director. Fill in the picture: a director of what? Where? What will life be like when you get there? How will it feel? When will you get your title? With which organisation?

State each of your goals as an affirmation

Use affirmations to support your goals. Develop action steps for them. An affirmation is an 'I' statement that uses the present tense – it reads as if you had already achieved your goal. For instance, a career affirmation might be:

'I am Director of Marketing for a major retailer at the London head office.'
'I remain cool and level-headed no matter what happens around me.'

Make a list of your goals then write out an affirmation for each. Read your affirmations at least once daily.

Goal success exercise

Some people don't like to set goals because if they do not meet them, they will feel they have failed.

Following is an exercise to clear away the ghosts of 'failures' (past or future).

In the space opposite, list every event you consider to have been a major personal failure. If the book is borrowed, make a separate list.

Now, cross out each individually with a thick, black line.

After all have been crossed out, tear out the page and throw the list away.

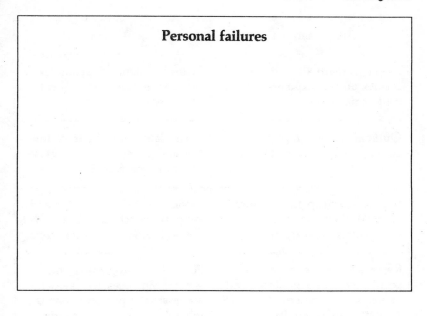

Personal failures

Involve your team in goal setting

Goals must reflect personal ownership in order to be meaningful. You cannot effectively and continuously strive toward someone else's goals if you have not accepted a personal stake in them. That's why you must 'own' the goals of your organisation if you are to attain them and motivate your team to accept and work towards achieving them.

The roles of team member and leader are outlined below. Circle those concepts with which you agree and are willing to try.

Team member	Leader
Helps to establish performance goals and standards. This is a 'self-contract' for achievement as well as a commitment to deliver a result for the team.	Ensures that team goals are achievable, but challenging enough to meet organisational needs and provide a sense of accomplishment.

Team member	Leader
Develops methods to measure results, and checkpoints for control purposes.	Helps to balance the complexity of measures and controls with value received.
Outlines the action required to accomplish goals and standards.	Participates with the team to test the action plan's validity against other alternatives.
Specifies participation required from colleagues or in other units within the organisation.	Reviews what cooperation and support are required and helps to obtain them if they are needed.
Reports progress as work is performed. Seeks guidance and assistance when needed. Adjusts plan as required.	Follows the progress of the work. Reinforces achievement and assists in problem-solving when indicated. Ensures that targets are met, or modified if circumstances so indicate.

These roles place the responsibility for performance on the appropriate team members. The leader concentrates on leading.

Getting organised

Stephanie Winston, a well-known consultant on managerial productivity and author of *The Organised Executive*, says, 'Getting organised is not an end in itself; it is a means to get where you want to be.'*

Table adapted from *Team Building: An Exercise in Leadership* by Robert B Maddux (Kogan Page).

The Organised Executive: New Ways to Manage Time, Paper and People by Stephanie Winston (Kogan Page).

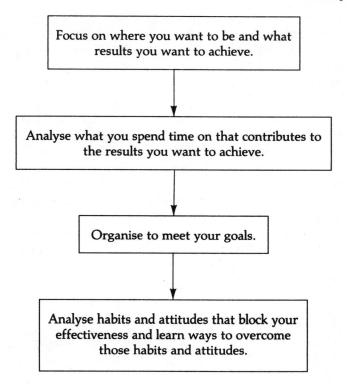

Focus on where you want to be and what results you want to achieve.

Analyse what you spend time on that contributes to the results you want to achieve.

Organise to meet your goals.

Analyse habits and attitudes that block your effectiveness and learn ways to overcome those habits and attitudes.

Leaders and time management

'If you want to make good use of your time, you've got to know what's most important and then give it all you've got.'

Lee Iacocca
President, Chrysler Corporation

Effective leaders do not travel at reckless speeds ... instead they:

- keep a steady pace;
- expect the unexpected;
- know how to delegate for results; and
- don't waste other people's time.

For an excellent book on this topic read *Make Every Minute Count* by Marion E Haynes (Kogan Page).

Time control begins with planning. Every work-related action you perform should take you closer to achieving your goals. These actions should also be prioritised according to the relative importance of your goals.

You should maintain a diary or desk journal that allows you to write action steps for your goals each day.

Set aside some time each week (ie first thing Monday morning) to go over your goals and decide action steps that need to be taken during the coming week. Schedule those steps as if they were appointments to be kept during the week.

Group common tasks together. For instance, try to set aside a specific time each day to make and return phone calls. This will help to eliminate some interruptions.

If you have to be away from your office for a meeting or appointment, identify any errands or other meetings you can schedule in that geographic area. This will eliminate wasted motion and reduce time spent travelling.

Watch out for time theft!

Q. What happens when employees don't know how to do their jobs, can't do their jobs because something prevents them, or don't want to do their jobs?

A. Employees become less productive. They commit 'time crime'.

Time crime is the disappearance of time at the company's expense. Time crime takes many forms. Do you recognise any of these? Tick those you have experienced:

☐ Extra time tacked on to breaks and/or lunch

☐ Frequent trips to the washroom

☐ Lengthy personal phone calls

☐ Work flow held up by other departments

Adapted from *How to Motivate People* by Twyla Dell (Kogan Page).

☐ Inappropriate staffing for the amount of work; too many or too few employees

☐ Low morale causing negative attitudes and group complaining sessions

☐ Procrastination.

If any of these time crimes regularly occur in your department, write out steps you can take to eliminate time crime from your department.

Ten commandments of time management

1. Plan your activities DAILY.
2. Do high priority actions FIRST.
3. Learn to delegate effectively.
4. Group similar activities to save time.
5. Learn how to handle interruptions efficiently.
6. Learn to say 'No' to non-critical tasks.
7. Eliminate inefficient habits.
8. Mark appointments, meetings, and deadlines in your diary and review it daily.
9. Do ONLY those tasks that are appropriate for your position.
10. Learn the difference between 'urgent' and 'important'.

'I would willingly stand at street corners, hat in hand, begging passers by to drop their unused minutes into it.'

Barnard Berenson
Art critic, as he neared
90 years of age

Leaders and meetings

Meetings that work
A recent study found that managers spend 17 hours a week in meetings, not counting the hours spent preparing for and recovering from meetings.

You don't have much control over other people's meetings, but you can control your own. Effective leaders cultivate the skills of a good meeting leader.

Meet before a meeting
Contact associates to garner support for ideas and lay any background you will need to defend your ideas and suggestions. Define who will make formal presentations at the meeting.

Plan an agenda
Identify the items to be discussed and distribute the agenda to attenders a few days before the meeting. Define how long the meeting should last and the length of time allotted to each speaker, if appropriate.

Prepare what you need for the meeting
If you need charts, numbers, reports, prepare them before you arrive and make sure they are in the room before the meeting starts. Test overhead projectors and other mechanical equipment to make sure it works properly before your attenders arrive.

Lead the meeting
Never lose control of the meeting. Arrive on time and start promptly. If someone tries to monopolise the meeting, suggest that you meet that person later for a private discussion. If the meeting goes off on a tangent, promptly bring it back on target.

How to delegate skilfully

Delegating
When you delegate intelligently, you not only exhibit leadership, you also develop the leadership skills of your employees. As a result, your job gets easier and your team becomes more productive.

For an excellent book on meetings, read *Effective Meeting Skills* by Marion E Haynes (Kogan Page).

> WHEN YOU DELEGATE,
> YOUR TEAM MEMBERS LEARN TO THINK LIKE
> LEADERS AND THE COMMITMENT AND ENERGY OF THE
> TEAM CAN INCREASE DRAMATICALLY

Effective delegation takes time, patience, and follow-up, but it is worth the effort. Delegation can motivate employees by giving them greater ownership in the organisation's productivity.
Delegate tasks when:

- You need more time for your work.
- You want to develop an employee's potential by delegating an assignment to him or her and observing the results.
- You need to restructure responsibilities to handle a heavy workload.

1. Select the project carefully
Make a list of assignments you feel can be delegated. These may be assignments that take too much of your time or that can be handled effectively by one of your employees. Most assignments should not require constant monitoring or follow-up.

2. Select the person for each task carefully
Consider all factors involved before selecting the person to whom you will delegate the project.

- What is the person's current workload?
- Will the task be accepted with enthusiasm?
- How will colleagues react?
- Will the employee have to be relieved of other responsibilities?

3. Prepare others for the change
Let employees in your department know that responsibility for each task has to be assigned to a colleague. Explain why the project was delegated.

4. Make the assignment thoughtfully
Go over the assignment carefully and use examples if possible.

Ask the employee if he or she understands the assignment. Ask the employee to repeat the assignment. Give the employee the opportunity to ask questions. Convey confidence in the way the employee will handle the new responsibility.

5. Follow up
Make yourself available to answer questions. Make suggestions when necessary but allow the employee freedom to manage the assignment. Compliment the employee when the task has been satisfactorily completed.

You can delegate authority, but you cannot delegate responsibility. As long as you are responsible, you must know how things are going.

Rate yourself as a delegator

Answer:
A. Usually
B. Sometimes
C. Seldom/Never

_____ 1. Do you take work home?

_____ 2. Do you work significantly longer hours than your staff?

_____ 3. Do you do the work of others because you can do it faster or better?

_____ 4. When you return to work from an absence, is your in-tray overflowing?

_____ 5. Do you continue to handle activities you had from previous jobs?

_____ 6. Do employees constantly interrupt you with questions about their projects or assignments?

_____ 7. Do you perform routine tasks others could easily handle?

_____ 8. Are you slow in meeting deadlines?

_____ 9. Do you feel the need to keep an eye on every activity in your unit?

_____ 10. Are you poor at setting priorities?

_____ 11. Are you uncomfortable when your employees don't have enough to do?

_____ 12. Do you hear criticism about your lack of delegation?

Note any items you answered with As and list areas you identify for improvement, eg I will do a better job of delegating tasks and training employees in order to eliminate interruptions.

1.

2.

3.

Decision-making and leadership

'Take time to deliberate, but when the time for action arrives, stop thinking and go in.'

Andrew Jackson

Most decisions involve an element of risk or uncertainty. No matter how much information you have, you cannot absolutely guarantee the outcome. Good leaders are good decision-makers even when it means taking a risk. The following steps will help you to develop your decision-making skills.

To become a more effective leader, I will:

- Identify available options before making a decision.
- Seek alternative options from team players.
- Encourage discussion over alternative options to stimulate creativity.
- Test each option against the situation.

- Identify who will assume responsibility for taking action based on a decision.
- Build in feedback mechanisms to assess the effectiveness of the decision.
- Make a decision.

CHAPTER 4
Leaders Are Problem Solvers

'If you don't believe that a puzzle has an answer, you'll never find it.'

Marvin Harris

Eight steps to effective problem-solving

1. Accept the problem as an opportunity to improve a situation.
2. Solicit the perceptions of those affected and identify differences.
3. Define the problem as specifically as possible.
4. Analyse why the problem exists, obtain facts, and identify barriers to resolution.
5. Brainstorm possible solutions.
6. Set criteria for the ultimate solution.
7. Select the solution that best meets the criteria.
8. Make the decision and install a means to measure the outcome.

Conflict resolution styles

There are five basic approaches to conflict resolution. They are summarised on page 48. Indicate the one you are most likely to use with followers with an F, your peers with a P, and with your manager, an S.

Style	Characteristic behaviour	User justification	F,P or S?
Avoidance	Non-confrontational. Ignores or passes over issues. Denies issues are a problem.	Differences too minor or too great to resolve. Attempts might damage relationships or create even greater problems.	
Accommodating	Agreeable, non-assertive behaviour. Cooperative even at the expense of personal goals.	Not worth risking damage to relationships or general disharmony.	
Win/Lose	Confrontational, assertive and aggressive. Must win at any cost.	Survival of the fittest. Must prove superiority. Most ethically or professionally correct.	
Compromising	Important all parties achieve basic goals and maintain good relationships. Aggressive but cooperative.	No one person or idea is perfect. There is more than one good way to do anything. You must give to get.	
Problem-solving	Needs of both parties are legitimate and important. High respect for mutual support. Assertive and cooperative.	When parties will openly discuss issues, a mutually beneficial solution can be found without anyone making a major concession.	

From *Team Building: An Exercise in Leadership* by Robert B Maddux (Kogan Page).

Conflict exercise

1. With whom do you have or have had a conflict?

(a) _____

(b) _____

(c) _____

2. What is or was the essence of the conflict?

(a) _____

(b) _____

(c) _____

Choose one of your conflicts identified above and complete the following. Describe the conflict resolution style which would have been most effective in the conflict you identified. Did you use it?

1. _____

2. _____

3. _____

Resolving conflict

Each of us operates from a unique perspective. Even if everyone has agreed on a goal or decision, disagreements can arise. When this happens it is essential to know how to resolve a conflict if you plan to be an effective leader. One stereotype you often hear about female employees is that they look for ways to avoid conflict. Strong leaders, male or female, need to be proficient at conflict resolution. Don't allow yourself to follow the stereotype.

Here are seven steps to help you resolve conflicts:

1. Schedule a meeting with the other party to discuss the situation.
2. When you meet, initiate a discussion that acknowledges there is a conflict.

3. Use 'I' statements to avoid accusations. Encourage the other party to use 'I' statements, too.
4. Ask direct questions that require the other party to talk about the situation.
5. Repeat what you are hearing. 'Based on what you've told me, this is how you see the situation.' This is a good way to confirm that you understand what you are hearing.
6. Tell the other party what you want as an outcome and ask what they want.
7. Agree to work towards a resolution and schedule a meeting, if required, to follow up the situation.

Managing difficult people

Difficult people are everywhere. They can be negative, irritating, seemingly impossible to manage, and create stress for everyone around them.

Sometimes it seems easier to avoid or 'work around' difficult people, but this is never a good long-term solution. If you learn to assess the person's behaviour and listen with genuine interest, it is possible to manage every difficult person effectively. Good leaders never avoid difficult management situations.

To help you learn how to manage difficult people, seven difficult personality types are listed below. In all seven cases, the behaviour of each type is described first, followed by effective action you can take to handle it.

Seven difficult personality types

1. ATTACKERS
Behaviour: Attackers assert their viewpoint forcefully. They require people to listen to what they say. They need room and time to blow off steam.
Your Action: Address the attacker by name and quietly, but firmly. Ask him or her to sit. Then listen carefully to what the attacker

---

A good book on the resolution of conflict is *Managing Disagreement Constructively* by Herbert S Kindler (Kogan Page).

has to say. Once calmed, the attacker usually becomes reasonable and may suggest valuable solutions. The worst coping behaviour on your part would be to return the attack.

2. EGOTISTS
Behaviour: Egotists also assert themselves but, unlike attackers, they may be subject experts.
Your action: Show honest respect for their knowledge, but don't become intimidated by it. Instead, capitalise on what they know by asking questions. Compliment them when they provide helpful information but make sure they know you are the leader.

3. SNEAKS
Behaviour: Sneaks take 'potshots' and often use sarcasm as a weapon.
Your action: Confront sneaks with direct questions and let them know you do not appreciate their sarcasm. Use positive reinforcement when possible to steer them towards becoming more of a team player.

4. VICTIMS
Behaviour: Victims see everything negatively. They act powerless and defeated, often whining about everyone and everything.
Your action: Ask them for suggestions to improve the situation. Have them state the negatives and address each logically and positively.

5. NEGATORS
Behaviour: Negators are usually suspicious of those in authority and believe that their way of doing things is the only way.
Your action: Let negators use their negative 'ammunition' in a group meeting, then let colleagues express their views about possible solutions. They will usually try to 'enlighten' negators that better solutions exist.

6. SUPER-AGREEABLE PEOPLE
Behaviour: Super-agreeable people have such a strong need to be liked that they do whatever you request at the expense of their

own needs. They will overcommit and often disappoint and frustrate everyone.

Your action: Monitor assignments to make sure they are not overworked.

7. UNRESPONSIVE PEOPLE

Behaviour: Unresponsive people are the most difficult people to manage. They are seemingly impossible to draw out.

Your action: Use open-ended questions that require more than a 'Yes' or 'No' answer. Wait for a response. Resist the urge to finish sentences for them. Follow up on actions assigned to them and give them assignments to present at future meetings.

Difficult people leadership exercise

List some difficult people you must work with and identify their dominant, difficult trait.

Person	Trait
1.	1.
2.	2.
3.	3.
4.	4.
5.	5.

Then review the strategies for each type of difficult person and summarise how you can more effectively approach each of these people in the future.

1.

2.

3.

4.

5.

Coaching and counselling

Effective leaders know how to coach and how to counsel employees. Even more important, they understand the differences between these skills and when to use each. Brief definitions of coaching and counselling are given below.

Counselling. A supportive process by a manager to help an employee define and work through personal problems that affect job performance.

Coaching. A directive process by a manager to train and orientate an employee to the realities of the workplace and to help the employee remove barriers to optimum work performance.

Counselling and coaching share many of the same skills. At times they may seem to overlap. When they do, remember the following diagrams. They will help you to differentiate these two processes.

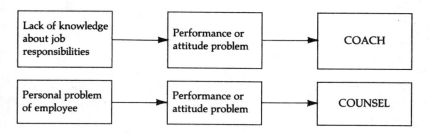

The benefits of coaching

Why should you improve your coaching skills if you are a leader? See if you agree with the authors by deciding which statements are true and which are false. Compare your answers with those of the authors on page 54.

Coaching

True   *False*

_____ _____ 1. Makes your job easier when employees build their skill levels.

_____ _____ 2. Enables greater delegation so you can have more time to truly manage versus 'do for'.

_____ _____ 3. Builds your reputation as a 'people developer'.

_____ _____ 4. Increases productivity when employees know what the goals are and how to achieve them.

_____ _____ 5. Develops sharing of leadership responsibilities.

_____ _____ 6. Positive recognition and feedback increase employee motivation and initiative.

_____ _____ 7. Increases likelihood of tasks being completed in a quality way.

_____ _____ 8. Avoids surprises and defensiveness in performance appraisals.

_____ _____ 9. Increases creativity and innovation of unit as employees feel safe to take risks.

_____ _____ 10. Increases team cohesiveness due to clarified goals and roles.

Answers. All ten statements are true.

The benefits of counselling

As a leader, why should you improve your counselling skills? Read each of the statements opposite. Do you think they are true or false? Check your opinion and compare it with that of the authors on page 55.

Counselling

True   *False*

—— —— 1. Improves productivity of your business unit when employees feel listened to and supported.

—— —— 2. Reduces turnover when employees feel they can vent their thoughts and feelings and deal with problems openly and constructively.

—— —— 3. Makes your job easier by giving you warning of resistance or problems that may occur following changes.

—— —— 4. Increases efficiency of your business unit when you understand the motives and needs of each employee and how he or she will react to organisational events.

—— —— 5. Reduces team conflict and preserves self-esteem when parties having conflict are really listened to.

—— —— 6. Helps you to solve problems before they occur.

—— —— 7. Improves your decision-making when everyone's ideas are heard and employees' strengths and abilities are complimented.

—— —— 8. Improves your career opportunities when you are known as a manager who can motivate employees and build constructive working relationships with bosses and peers.

—— —— 9. Increases self-knowledge and personal satisfaction in your job.

—— —— 10. Improves your self-confidence.

Answers. If you thought all ten statements were true, then you are right.

The art of feedback and using 'I' messages

Leaders understand how important feedback is. They also know, to be effective, it must be specific. It should also convey your true feelings. When delivering critical messages, it is especially important to let your employee know exactly how you feel about the situation – otherwise you are not being honest. For example, if one of your staff is continually late, you could pass the buck by saying: 'My boss has noticed you are not always on time for work and asked me to let you know this is against company regulations.' This would be transparent management, where you simply allowed a message from a higher authority to 'pass through' you to your employee. A more effective approach would be an 'I' message similar to the following:

'When you are late for work, I feel angry because others must do more to make up for you. Is there some reason you can't be on time?'

'I' messages are helpful because the person you are addressing feels less defensive. 'I feel ... (annoyed, angry, hurt, upset)' or 'In my opinion, I believe, I think ...' give more direct feedback.

Rewrite the following using 'I' messages.

Example:
'You never pay attention to my instructions.'
'Based on your last report, I feel you are not paying enough attention to my instructions. Do you agree?'

1. You always make me cross.

2. You really hurt my feelings.

3. You are too bossy.

Talking about how you feel

Women often stifle their feelings because they are afraid of being branded as too emotional. Being emotional is perfectly acceptable, as long as it is expressed appropriately. That's what 'I' messages allow you to do.

You must identify what you are feeling as specifically as possible. Ask yourself, 'What am I feeling – mad, sad, glad, or scared?' This question will help you to identify your feelings quickly and accurately.

The following vocabulary of emotions will help you better to identify and express your feelings in a direct, open, and honest manner.

Mad	Sad	Glad	Scared	Combination
irritated	unhappy	pleased	anxious	guilty
annoyed	disappointed	happy	worried	jealous
angry	despondent	joyful	fearful	frustrated
put down	blue	delighted	concerned	embarrassed
furious	hurt	effervescent	afraid	uncomfortable
miffed	grieved	comfortable	nervous	confused
upset	down	high	inhibited	perplexed
cross	lonely	excited	uncertain	torn

Add your own:

Mad	Sad	Glad	Scared	Combination

How to use positive anger

Leaders sometimes feel frustration or disappointment and respond with anger. Effectively expressing anger is difficult for many women who were reared to 'turn the other cheek' or 'be nice'. Often women don't believe that anger is a natural, honest feeling and don't realise that it can be an important safety valve.

Expressing anger can work for you or against you, depending on how you express it and with whom.

'If you are patient in one moment of anger, you will escape a hundred days of sorrow.'

Chinese proverb

Use anger to gain attention and to make a point if you normally handle situations coolly and professionally and if you are acting from conviction for something significant that benefits your organisation – for instance, fighting for a project you deeply believe in.

Some techniques for expressing anger productively and effectively are:

- Admit your angry feelings to yourself.
- Take deep breaths to calm yourself.
- If you begin to lose control 'drop' your pen (or take some similar momentary action) and as you bend over to get it, regain your composure.
- Take a break and do something physically vigorous or highly creative. When you engage in physical or mental exercise, you help to dissipate your anger.
- Prepare to confront the person or situation that caused you to feel angry. Once things get 'aired', things usually improve.

Tantrums and outbursts should be few and far between, or people will classify you as a difficult person. But if you lose control and 'blow up', cool off, then apologise – not for how you feel, but for your outburst.

'Anybody can become angry – that is easy. But to be angry with the right person, to the right degree, at the right time, for the right reason, and in the right way – that is not easy.'

Aristotle

'Stress busters'

Leaders often feel stress. Women leaders are particularly vulnerable because they often carry heavy workloads both on the job *and* at home.

Before you can act effectively at home or on the job, you must be able to control stress.

Use the following 'stress busters' whenever you feel your stress level rising.

- *Be present.* You can only live in the moment. Worrying about the past or future is not productive. When you concentrate on the present, you don't allow time for stressful fretting.
- *Grow, or let go.* When you are criticised, don't take it personally. Analyse it. Does the criticism repeat criticism you have heard previously? If so, perhaps it is valid and points out an area that needs work. If not, and if you believe the criticism is unjust, let it go. You can't change some people's minds if they choose to be unfair.
- *Do your personal best* and don't compare your performance with others. Trust yourself and your abilities.
- *Don't let tensions build up* inside until you feel like bursting. Get another person's opinion to help you put the situation in perspective.
- *Your life isn't the job.* At least it shouldn't be. When your work life takes a turn for the worst, rely on your home life and personal relationships to bolster you. And vice versa.
- *Expand your world.* Exercise, take up a hobby, go to a film, plan regular evenings out with a friend or loved one.

Tips to overcome stress

At work	At home
Take short breaks	Develop leisure interests
Add variety to your duties	Maintain personal relationships
Develop a support system	Leave your work at the office
Keep yourself detached	Keep physically fit
Develop positive work habits	Talk and play with loved ones
Encourage positive feedback	Encourage open communication

CHAPTER 5
Developing Personal Power

Balancing home and career

One of your most difficult challenges is to balance your career and your personal life. You want to establish a smooth flow between the two to be truly successful. This requires you to develop personal power.

Balancing a family and career can challenge the best leader. Avoid falling into the Superwoman trap by learning to treat domestic arrangements as management challenges, not personal crises.

- Hire household help if you need it.
- Accept the fact that many little things just won't get done.
- Learn to be imperfect. It can be most freeing.
- Develop a sense of humour.

Developing a sense of personal power involves developing a belief in yourself. You should believe that you can go after what you want and that you have the ability to reach your goals in your own way.

A powerful woman leader empowers others and provides a safe environment for them to express their opinions. The personally powerful leader encourages her subordinates to set goals, express themselves openly, and be important contributors to the work unit. Her employees feel supported and acknowledged.

You develop a sense of personal power by developing authority, accessibility, assertiveness, a positive image, and solid communication habits. We will look at each of these traits briefly in following pages.

1. Authority
Authority is inner confidence – a trust in your skills and abilities. Authority begins inside, with an attitude of 'I can do it; I deserve success'. This attitude radiates outwardly as you assert your rights, as you ask for what you need and want, and as you develop a willingness to give to others and yourself.

Many women tend to discount their successes and are often embarrassed by proclaiming their talents and strengths.

The image of Rocky bouncing around the ring, arms upraised in victory, is a male image. But women must stop denigrating their skills and talents; they must feel comfortable with the power they have earned.

2. Assertiveness: a key skill
It would be nice if you could simply decide to go down the road marked 'Assertive' and live your life without straying from the path. Women leaders must learn to hold their own in a positive way by learning assertiveness.

Real life is full of twists and turns and *no one is consistently assertive*. All of us use the three basic behaviour styles described below depending on the situation and personal factors. The good news is that *we can learn to become more assertive more of the time*.

1. *Non-assertive behaviour* is passive and indirect. It communicates a message of inferiority. By being non-assertive we allow the wants, needs, and rights of others to be more important than our own. Non-assertive behaviour helps to create 'win-lose' situations. A person behaving non-assertively will lose while allowing others to win (or at best be disregarded). Following this road leads to being a victim, not a winner.

2. *Aggressive behaviour* is more complex. It can be either active or passive. Aggression can be direct or indirect, honest or dishonest – but it always communicates an impression of superiority and disrespect. By being aggressive we put our wants, needs, and rights above those of others. We attempt to get our way by not

allowing others a choice. Aggressive behaviour is usually inappropriate because it violates the rights of others. People behaving aggressively may 'win' by making sure others 'lose' – but in doing so set themselves up for retaliation. No one likes a bully.

3. *Assertive behaviour* is active, direct, and honest. It communicates an impression of self-respect and respect for others. By being assertive we view our wants, needs, and rights as equal with those of others. We work towards 'win-win' outcomes. An assertive person wins by influencing, listening, and negotiating, so that others choose to cooperate willingly. This behaviour leads to success without retaliation and encourages honest, open relationships!

Here are some guidelines you can follow to increase your assertive leadership skills.

● Make time for yourself. Assert your right to take care of your own needs. This helps you to develop a healthy self-respect.
● Ask for help when you need it. Become a team player and let others know you do not work in a vacuum.
● Say 'No' without feeling guilty.
● Express your feelings openly. This involves risk-taking and demonstrates a high level of integrity.
● Request feedback as a way to grow and learn. This will develop an openness to change.
● Ask for what you need and want. Focus on your goals, developing a sense of purpose and commitment.
● Look for win-win situations.

3. Accessibility

You have probably heard the adage about 'being in the right place at the right time'. It is true, and effective leaders know how to make it happen. People do business with people they know, and the powerful woman leader is a master networker. By learning to develop skills as a team player, it is possible to increase visibility. Good networkers also give themselves a valuable circle of people from whom to seek information and support.

Adapted from *How to Develop Assertiveness* by Sam R Lloyd (Kogan Page).

You probably have more contacts than you realise. Imagine yourself as the hub of a wheel, surrounded by spokes of contacts. List every key person you know and every organisation you belong to in a graphic similar to the one shown below. Make sure your list takes into account anyone or any organisation that can help you reach your goals. Establish a goal to contact at least three people on your list each week to maintain contact.

FINANCIAL CONTACTS   PERSONAL CONTACTS
_____   _____
_____   _____
_____   _____

SOCIAL CONTACTS ——————— YOU ——————— SPIRITUAL CONTACTS
_____   _____
_____   _____
_____   _____

COMMUNITY CONTACTS   CAREER CONTACTS
_____   _____
_____   _____
_____   _____

Accessibility also means letting your world – your organisation, religious unit, industry or professional group or community – know who you are. Volunteer, write articles, join committees. To become successful, you must network, network, network!

- Join your industry association.
- Subscribe to trade publications.
- Join business organisations such as your local Chamber of Commerce.
- Write articles for magazines and newspapers.
- Add your own _____ .

4. Image
You communicate inner authority to others through your image.

Effective leaders communicate their authority. Are you projecting the image consistent with a strong leader? Is your voice firm or little-girl cute? Worse, do you whine?

Is your speech littered with slang or do you hesitate with vocal 'uhhhhhhs?'

If your job requires telephone contact, tape record telephone conversations (with the permission of the person you are calling) to monitor your speech patterns and tone of voice.

When you meet people, make direct eye contact when you speak to them. Keep your handshake firm and friendly.

You can never fully erase a first impression, so it is very important to project the best possible image the first time around.

'Stand tall. The difference between towering and cowering is totally a matter of inner posture. It's got nothing to do with height, it costs nothing and it's more fun.'

Malcolm Forbes

5. Solid communication habits

Pay attention to how you speak and how you act as you speak. Often non-verbal signals say more than words do. Make sure your body isn't saying something different from your mouth.

Practise the following good communication habits until they become second nature:

- Look people in the eye.
- Keep your facial expression consistent with your message.
- Stand erect and move energetically.
- Speak with an even pace and enunciate clearly.
- Use only body movements and gestures necessary to make your point, but no more.

Practise projecting authority. You will not be accepted as a leader until you learn to communicate clearly and directly – in writing, in speaking, in listening and through the professional image you present. It is all a form of communication.

A good book on improving your voice is *Speak with Confidence* by Meribeth Bunch (Kogan Page).

CHAPTER 6
Summary – Having It All

A leader

- Keeps her objectives clear and attainable;
- Balances and limits tasks to avoid harmful stress;
- Assigns priorities for maximum pay-offs;
- Evaluates her behaviour to ensure it is appropriate;
- Revises and changes her plans as necessary;
- Visualises achievement of her goals;
- Knows the difference between failure and learning;
- Has convictions and acts on them;
- Has fun.

The benefits of being a woman leader

As you cultivate personal power, professional and positional power follow. You create 'win-win' situations for yourself and those around you. By embracing and expressing your power to the world, you become the powerful person you want to be.

Your life is more interesting and satisfying because you will have opportunities to grow. You will experience things such as travel, interesting classes, and seminars. Your horizons will expand in all directions.

You will meet more diverse and interesting people. With greater responsibility and visibility, you will be more in demand. Virtually every organisation is looking for women with strong leadership abilities.

You will also look better! When a woman feels successful with her accomplishments, she adds a confident aura that makes her more attractive.

You will enjoy a greater income and the increased freedom that goes with it.

- Your self-esteem will be enhanced.
- Your career opportunities will multiply.
- You become more comfortable with power.

All the above are reasons for you to become the best woman leader possible. It's up to you. Good luck!

Professional development - summary review

Answer these final questions as honestly as possible. They will help to guide you when applying what you have learned from this book. Briefly write your responses in the space provided.

1. What are your personal career objectives?

2. What new skills have you learned recently which will help you to achieve your goals?

3. What training have you taken to enhance your professionalism?

4. What training do you plan to take this year?

5. What professional literature have you read in the past few months?

6. What networks or organisations do you now belong to?

7. What are your plans for professional development in the next year?

8. How do you intend to apply what you have learned from this book to your leadership skills?

Reading List

The following titles are recommended:

Deal, Terrence and Kennedy, Allen. *Corporate Cultures: The Rites & Rituals of Corporate Life*. Addison-Wesley (1984)

Fisher, Roger & Ury, William L. *Getting to Yes*. Hutchinson (1983)

Friedman, M.D., Meyer and Ulmer, Diane. *Treating Type-A Behaviour. You and Your Heart*. Michael Joseph (1985)

Garfield, Charles A. *Peak Performers: The New Heroes of American Business*. Hutchinson (1986)

Gilligan, Carol. *In a Different Voice: Psychological Theory and Women's Development*. Harvard University Press. (1982)

Kanter, Rosabeth M. *Change Masters: Corporate Entrepreneurs at Work*. Allen & Unwin (1984)

Lakein, A. *How to Get Control of Your Time and Your Life*. Gower (1985)

Oncken, William. *Managing Management Time: Who's Got the Monkey?* Prentice-Hall (1985)

Peel, Malcolm. *How to Make Meetings Work*. Kogan Page (1988)

Peters, Tom and Austin, Nancy. *Passion for Excellence*. Fontana (1986)

Robert, Marc. *Managing Conflict from the Inside out*. Learning Concepts, USA (1983)

Siegel, Bernie S. *Love, Medicine & Miracles*. Century (1986)

Better Management Skills from Kogan Page
Effective Meeting Skills: How to Make Meetings More Productive, Marion E Haynes

Effective Performance Appraisals, Robert B Maddux

Effective Presentation Skills, Steve Mandel

The Fifty-Minute Supervisor: A Guide for the Newly Promoted, Elwood N Chapman

How to Communicate Effectively, Bert Decker

How to Develop a Positive Attitude, Elwood N Chapman

How to Motivate People, Twyla Dell

Make Every Minute Count: How to Manage Your Time Effectively, Marion E Haynes

Managing Disagreement Constructively, Herbert S Kindler

Successful Negotiation, Robert B Maddux

Team Building: An Exercise in Leadership, Robert B Maddux